GALVESTON
A CITY ON STILTS

A raised fence can be seen awaiting fill on the south side of Broadway between Twenty-seventh and Twenty-eighth Streets. The family on the porch is also featured on the cover image.

ON THE FRONT COVER: Residents between Twenty-seventh and Twenty-eighth Streets at Broadway watch the progress of the city's grade-raising efforts.

ON THE BACK COVER: A boy stands in one of the pipes used to pump in filling material to raise the level of Galveston. The pipes were 42 inches in diameter. Each 12-foot length weighed about one ton.

GALVESTON
A CITY ON STILTS

JODI WRIGHT-GIDLEY AND JENNIFER MARINES

Published by Arcadia Publishing
Charleston SC, Chicago IL, Portsmouth NH, San Francisco CA

Printed in the United States of America

Library of Congress Catalog Card Number: 2008925026

For all general information contact Arcadia Publishing at:
Telephone 843-853-2070
Fax 843-853-0044
E-mail sales@arcadiapublishing.com
For customer service and orders:
Toll-Free 1-888-313-2665

Visit us on the Internet at www.arcadiapublishing.com

To photographer Zeva B. Edworthy and his family, for allowing us a glimpse into a segment of Galveston's history, and to those who believe in Galveston's future.

CONTENTS

ACKNOWLEDGMENTS

The Galveston County Historical Museum is a joint project of the Galveston County Commissioners Court and the Galveston Historical Foundation, a 501(c)3 nonprofit. The museum opened in 1976 through the generosity of the Mary Moody Northen Endowment. Numerous staff and volunteers have contributed to the institution, which strives to further the knowledge of, and foster an appreciation for, the history and heritage of Galveston County.

We are grateful to the donors of this wonderful collection of photographs, Judith Edworthy Wray, as well as her husband, John, and her sister Norma Jane Edworthy White, whose generosity made this book possible. We would like to thank the following for their assistance with this project: W. Dwayne Jones, Brian Davis, Jamie Durham, and John Schaumberg of the Galveston Historical Foundation; Casey Edward Greene and the staff of the Galveston and Texas History Center (Rosenberg Library); Moody Mansion Museum; and Alecya Gallaway of the Galveston County Historical Commission. Stan Blazyk; Lew Fincher; Brian R. Jarvinen; Chris Landsea, Ph.D.; Bill Read; and Wil Shaffer, Ph.D., contributed their knowledge of hurricane history. We also appreciate our volunteer museum committee members Dayle Delancy, Ph.D.; Bill Foley; Jeannie Thielemann; Linda Turner; Cheryl Vaiani, Ph.D.; and Heather Green Wooten, Ph.D., as well as the Laffite Society members Dorothy McDonald Karilanovic, Lou Graves MacBeth, and Jim Nonus. Staff members Jackie Soileau and Juan Olivarez also were very helpful during this project. We would like to express appreciation to three special assistants: Kathy Marines, Joy Wright, and Jimmie Gidley. Finally, we would like to thank our families and friends for their unending support that sustains us through each museum project.

Every photograph featured in this publication is from the museum's collection. Unless otherwise noted, they are part of the Zeva B. Edworthy Collection donated by Judith Edworthy Wray.

Broadway East from 16th St.

This 1908 photograph depicts the stately houses on Broadway, complete with new landscaping after the grade raising.

Photographer Zeva B. Edworthy (1883–1954) worked in Galveston from about 1904 to 1910. In 1905, Frank Patten, the librarian of Rosenberg Library, took a collection of Edworthy photographs along on a trip to the eastern United States. One man commented on the images, "They are as fine as any that have been taken in the city. The group [of photographs] showing the library and that of scenes along Broadway are especially fine, and would prove a great advertisement to Galveston if published in book form with descriptive matter."

PREFACE

Hundreds of large photographs taken 100 years ago in Galveston, Texas, recently came to light after having been stored for decades in distant closets. My father, Zeva Bradshaw Edworthy, born in Kansas in 1883, was the photographer. Soon after graduating in 1904 from Washburn College in Topeka, he moved to Galveston and became a commercial photographer. He had a sense of adventure, was familiar with the relatively new art of photography, and, of course, he knew about the disastrous 1900 hurricane and flood damage in the city. This challenged him to document the rebuilding of Galveston and the construction of its gigantic seawall.

In 1911, he moved to Houston, engaged in real estate, and also traveled extensively, taking scenic photographs. He served in the U.S. Coastal Guard Artillery during World War I and later moved to Cisco, Texas, where in 1922 he married Cleo Christine Mancill and they moved to Colorado. Later he earned his divinity degree at Northwestern University. Finally they settled in Charleston, West Virginia, where he became director of religious education for the West Virginia Council of Churches, a position he held until his retirement in 1952.

I was born in 1929, and three years later, my sister Norma Jane was born. Our parents seldom told us much about their early lives. Family history wasn't much of an interest to us, unfortunately. We were a happy, although frugal, family during the Depression and World War II. Meals always began with a blessing; we attended church and Sunday school regularly. Our father was busy at the office or traveling around the state conducting religious education workshops and was a fine handyman and gardener. Photography continued to be a part of his life for many years. He always seemed more like a grandfather, however, as he was much older than Mother.

My sister and I have vivid memories of our father in his basement photography darkroom, where he bent over the tray of pungent "hypo" bringing photographs magically into existence. My sister and I ultimately went to college, married, moved away, and raised our own families. We were never aware that Daddy had worked as a professional photographer in Galveston, although Mother told us that he had lived there "for a few years."

He died in 1954, and my mother lived for many more years. Shortly before she died, she asked me in a letter, "Did you ever see the photographs Daddy took in Galveston years ago? The next time you come back to visit me, let's look at them together. I want you to have them when I die." We did not have that opportunity. Her health declined, and she passed away in 1998.

I inherited the photographs and discovered them in an enormous album locked in Mother's bedroom closet. The leather cover was disintegrating, many pages were torn, but the photographs themselves were in surprisingly good condition. I brought it back to my home in Colorado; however, my professional work schedule and family responsibilities caused me to forget about the photographs until several years later. Then, in 2005, I opened the album again, and my husband and I spent hours studying the fascinating pictures. We realized they needed proper preservation. I also wanted to return them to Galveston. I contacted the Galveston County Historical Museum early in 2006 and, subsequently, donated the collection of 340 photographs to the museum.

In June 2007, the museum opened A City on Stilts: Galveston, 1902–1912. The exhibit featured more than 75 dramatically enlarged digital copies of the Edworthy photographs, enhanced with many artifacts of the period from the museum's own collection. Thus, my father's photographs, depicting rare scenes of Galveston's resurrection after the 1900 disaster, finally have returned.

—Judith Edworthy Wray
November 2007

Four months before the storm, Galveston celebrated San Jacinto Day with a downtown parade on April 21, 1900. The float depicts the Texas Heroes Monument, still located at Broadway and Twenty-fifth Street, which was dedicated during the ceremonies in honor of the famous battle. (Courtesy of David Winters.)

INTRODUCTION

Adventurers and pirates first explored the island later named Galveston before it became an established port under the Mexican government in 1825. City leaders developed the wharves and railroads as the population of the town increased. Being the only deepwater port between New Orleans and Tampico, Mexico, Galveston supplied Texas and the western United States with essential goods that fueled development of the entire nation. By 1899, the town had become a bustling commercial center of wharves, cotton warehouses, banks, and stores. With more millionaires per capita than any other U.S. city in the late 1800s, many of the prosperous population of about 38,000 enjoyed living in elegant homes, purchasing the finest imported goods, and dining in European-inspired restaurants. Galveston was the first in the state to have telegraphs, telephones, and electric-powered houses, streetlights, and trolleys.

No contemporary Galvestonian would have predicted that on September 8, 1900, the city would be devastated. Dr. Isaac M. Cline, chief of the Galveston Weather Bureau, warned people on the island that a hurricane was approaching, but little could be done as the storm reached the island. Throughout the night, water slowly rose to cover the entire island, and winds reached more than 120 miles per hour. People attempted to find shelter in churches, hospitals, private homes, and hotels. As Sunday morning dawned, Galvestonians witnessed the widespread destruction that was unlike anything that had ever occurred in an American city. Two-thirds of the city's buildings were gone. The storm deposited a huge debris pile measuring about three miles long and two stories tall. At least 6,000 deaths on the island were documented, although historians have agreed that the amount must have been higher.

On September 14, 1900, the *Galveston Daily News* printed:

> The sorrows of the past few days are overwhelming and we all feel them and will continue to feel them so long as we live. . . . Wherever they sleep . . . we will love their memories and recall as long we live the unspeakable and mysterious tragedy which destroyed them. But it must be remembered that we have more than 30,000 living, and many of these are children too young to have their lives and energies paralyzed by the disaster which has overtaken us. Our homes must be rebuilt, our schools repaired, and the natural advantages of the port must sooner or later receive our earnest attention. We have loved Galveston too long and too well to desert her in the hour of misfortune. . . . We must look to the light ahead.

Eventually, city leaders developed an ambitious plan to minimize the forces of the gulf by constructing a wall against the sea, raising the level of 500 city blocks to deter flooding, and linking the island to the mainland with a reliable concrete bridge to facilitate evacuation. These unprecedented efforts required great community support and determination. While the grade was raised beneath them, houses were perched on stilts and residents made their way through town on elevated boardwalks. Galveston became a "city on stilts."

In the wake of the 1900 Storm, a damaged house sits in the middle of the road at Fourteenth Street and Avenue K. (Courtesy of David Winters.)

This neighborhood, at Market and Twelfth Streets, is featured in a film made by Albert E. Smith in the days following the 1900 Storm. Smith was contracted by famed inventor Thomas Edison. (Courtesy of David Winters.)

Robert, Ripley, and Noble recommended the concrete seawall be 3 miles long and 17 feet above average low tide, which was 1.3 feet above the highest water in the 1900 Storm. It would be 16 feet wide at the bottom and 5 feet wide at the top with a concave face to deflect the force of the waves. It would rest on timber piling driven into the sand with a 27-foot-wide apron of riprap to protect the front. The original portion would stretch from the South Jetty at Eighth Street, then south down Sixth Street before curving west, protecting the island to Thirty-ninth Street. The federal government would then extend the wall to Fifty-third Street to protect Fort Crockett.

OPPOSITE: The caption on this image reads, "Picture from old negative—Showing Galveston beach at foot of 22nd st. and East. This shows houses on low beach level. The city grade prior to the wonderful raising by filling city up to level of seawall & raising all houses, buildings, etc." The negative was presumably retouched by the photographer.

ONE

A WALL AGAINST THE SEA

In 1886, a commission of city leaders considered building a seawall to protect Galveston Island. Citizens rejected the proposal because it seemed costly and unnecessary. In the wake of the massive flooding caused by the 1900 Storm, the need for a seawall could no longer be denied. On November 22, 1901, the city appointed a board of engineers to make recommendations on how to keep Galveston safe from future overflows by raising the city's grade and building a breakwater, or seawall, along the gulf. Board members were Brig. Gen. H. M. Robert, former head of the Army Corps of Engineers and famous for publishing *Robert's Rules of Order*; Alfred Noble of Chicago, who had helped design that city's breakwater and raising; and H. C. Ripley, who had lived in Galveston and was familiar with its idiosyncrasies and available resources. They delivered their report on January 25, 1902. In addition to a 17-foot, 3-mile-long seawall, they recommended that the island's grade should be raised, its southern edge matching the seawall's height before gently sloping toward the bay.

The seawall's lower foundation began with four rows of round wooden pilings 3.5 feet apart. Made of longleaf yellow pine from East Texas, each round pile was 12 inches in diameter and 40 to 44 feet long. A tight row of sheet piling was driven just behind the first row. Three planks thick and 24 feet long, the sheet piling protected the round piles and thus the seawall from undermining. The first carloads of these supports arrived from Beaumont on October 27, 1902, nearly a month late. At 2:00 p.m., the first pile was driven at the foot of Fifteenth Street. It took 20 minutes to reach the island's hard clay foundation. Forty men and four machines worked whenever the weather allowed. The image above left shows all five rows of piling in place. In the background, a machine pours concrete to continue forming the wall's understructure. The image at bottom left shows a pile driver placing the sheet piling.

Workers dug a trench 3 feet deep and just over 16 feet wide along the line of pilings. The "little mixer," which rode on rails straddling the trench, poured concrete made of crushed granite, cement, sand, and water to form the seawall's upper foundation. The wet concrete was firmly tamped around the pilings. Three continuous depressions were created to be used later when connecting to the upper wall. Steel reinforcing rods, 10 feet long and 4 feet apart, were held in position by light ropes. Notice the rods also were useful as a hat and coat rack as seen in the lower left corner.

Four railroad tracks ran behind the future seawall. The railcars on the track closest to the building site contained giant blocks of granite, some weighing half a ton or more, that would eventually form the riprap apron meant to protect the wall from the tide. This buffer was placed before the upper portion of the seawall itself. Here a powerful steam crane moves the granite into place while sitting atop the wall's solid foundation. The railroad company assigned 200 cars to this project. Trainloads of granite arrived almost daily from a quarry 200 miles away in central Texas. Half of the stones were required to weigh at least 200 pounds each, and one-fifth were required to be 1,000 pounds or more. Nothing less than 18 pounds was to be used. The larger stones were placed at the ground with the smaller pieces filling the gaps to make as solid a surface as possible. The granite riprap extended 27 feet toward the gulf.

The "big mixer" produced 300 cubic yards of concrete per day. It had two steam cranes. The one at left carried the granite, cement, and sand from the neighboring boxcars and emptied them into the mixer's open mouth, where they were mixed with water to form concrete. The arm on the right carried the fresh concrete to wooden molds. In these photographs, one can see completed monoliths alternating with open wall forms.

To avoid cracking as a result of contraction, expansion, and settling of the concrete, the upper portion of the seawall was built in pieces. Each section was 60 feet long and connected to its neighbor by a tongue-and-groove system. One section was built per day and required seven days to dry. Seven alternating sections were built, then the intervening ones. The photograph at top left shows an incomplete seawall form being dwarfed by a concrete mixer. The photograph at bottom left shows a section with its wooden form still partially intact. Notice that granite riprap is being used to help brace the form.

GALVESTON WITH SEA WALL AND
LEVEL RAISED BY FILLING.

This painting by Julius Stockfleth (1857–1935) from about 1904 shows the seawall's original curve up Sixth Street. It became the basis of a very popular postcard of the day. In 1921, the wall was extended eastward to protect Fort San Jacinto and the East End Flats.

Completed July 29, 1904, the initial seawall was 17,593 feet long, or about 3.5 miles, and weighed 40,000 pounds per foot. Used in its production were 5,200 railway carloads of crushed granite, 1,800 carloads of sand, 1,000 carloads of concrete, 1,200 carloads of round wooden pilings, 4,000 carloads of wooden sheet pilings, 3,700 carloads of stone riprap, and 5 carloads of reinforcing steel. This great bulwark is now over 10 miles long after several extensions.

Almost immediately after its completion, Seawall Boulevard became a popular promenade and the site of numerous amusements, restaurants, and events.

A scene at Galveston Beach, The Playground of The South.

At the "Playground of the South," visitors could swim in the ocean, promenade along the seawall, and take a thrill ride at the amusement parks.

OPPOSITE: "When one enters the water it is to put aside dignity and conventionality and return to the freedoms of childhood. . . . If the ladies get their hair wet, giving them a disheveled appearance, nothing is thought of it. . . . There is more pure democracy in the water at Galveston beach than in any other spot in Texas," stated one *Galveston Daily News* reporter. Bathhouses, like the Breakers in this image, provided visitors with wool bathing suits for swimming.

THE PLAYGROUND OF TEXAS

Commerce was Galveston's primary force for early development, but almost equally as important became its status as a seaside resort. By the late 1800s, the town was known for amusements such as roller skating and carnivals. The construction projects, including the seawall, grade raising, and causeway, also propelled the town's shift to a tourist economy. After the first section of seawall was completed in 1904, the beach area underwent a boom of new construction to entice tourists. With a growing number of vehicles on the road, people were looking for driving destinations. In the summer of 1907, the *Galveston Daily News* boasted that Galveston had two amusement parks, the Electric Park and the Chutes Park, along with Murdoch's and Breakers bathhouses and numerous hotels and guesthouses: "All these together with Galveston's famous beach, should and will give every visitor his money's worth, and the season just opening will unquestionably be the greatest in the history of the city."

Away from the beaches, Galveston also offered parks, a golf club, and numerous planned special events. The rich array of social activities contributed to the town's dynamic appeal.

The Galveston Seawall and Grade Raising Monument was installed in 1904 to commemorate the two epic projects. The pair of round-top granite pillars became a gathering place for visitors at Twenty-third Street and Seawall Boulevard.

The *Galveston Daily News* reported in January 1901 that George Murdoch would begin construction for a new bathhouse to be ready by the summer season. Murdoch had every confidence in the future of Galveston, despite the tragedy of 1900, when he stated, "I don't want it said when they arrive that there is no place of recreation in the city. The new bathhouse will be strictly up to date and every detail has been planned for comfort."

Opening night for the Galveston Electric Park was May 25, 1906. The owner treated the public to free admission and a display of 6,000 electric lights and 212 flags swirling in the breeze. The "Coney Island of the South" was the largest resort in the western United States.

The Galveston Electric Park featured a children's area, a penny arcade, concerts, vaudeville shows, and a large variety of refreshments. One newspaper report boasted that the Mexican restaurant employed competent cooks directly from Mexico who used authentic ovens. Author James Hanna remembers visiting the amusement park and being especially enthralled by the miniature steam railway: "This was all that was needed to inspire my brothers and me to convert our backyard into an amusement park. With a large supply of old lumber . . . we had constructed a bicycle shoot-the-shoot and a railroad that started from an elevated platform at the top of the high board fence."

Throughout June 1906, midweek excursion trains brought people from Houston to the amusement park. Rides such as the Sea Swing and the Human Laundry, along with a roller coaster and a Ferris wheel, were great thrills for the visitors. One reporter who visited the park in August 1907 had difficulty finding a place to sit. He spoke with a young man who rode the Electric Swing 11 consecutive times and needed to "find a spot where his weary frame could be adjusted to a sitting position and that after this continuous trifling with centrifugal force an equal period was spent in the ferris wheel to counteract the effects of the spree."

The Nickelodeon played an assortment of "moving picture shows." Titles included *Baby's Peril* and *Miss Killarney's Swimming Lesson*. The movie business was going through phenomenal growth and development at this time. There was a high demand for comedies and dramas suitable for family viewing at rates affordable to lower classes.

Several theaters and exhibits were also featured at the park. "The City of Yesterday" was a stage and light show about the San Francisco earthquake of April 1906, which occurred just before the park opened. "Naval Battles of the World" and the "Creation of the World" were also special features.

Sold by Gust Feist.

In May 1907, the long-awaited water park opened as an addition to the Galveston Electric Park. Manager Charles Niemeyer had experience in similar parks in Chicago. It had taken about a year to obtain all the machinery and to assemble the water park. The 1,000-foot-long waterway was propelled by a waterwheel. Rides included Shoot-the-Chutes, Figure 8, Carryall, and the Mystic Chutes.

Galveston committees planned several special events to draw visitors, including the Cotton Carnival, National Maritime Day, and the Water Carnival. In 1911, one event even provided childcare services so parents could enjoy the festivities without their children. Nurses staffed a special area where children were left to play with toys in sandboxes. Each child wore an identification tag.

The drive along the seawall was known as one of the most scenic in the state. By 1911, traffic on the road during special events became an issue. During the annual Cotton Carnival that year, new parking arrangements were made on Sixty-first Street so automobiles could more easily enter and exit. Promoters added automobile races to the carnival.

The prospect of building a large resort hotel on the beach was seen as "a broad spirit of patriotism and civic pride." The opening of the Hotel Galvez, known as the "Queen of the Gulf," in June 1911 solidified the role Galveston would play as a tourist attraction. Manager J. F. Letton described the new hotel as "Good enough for everybody; not too good for anybody." The "homey" rooms all looked out over the gulf and beyond to the numerous bathhouses and amusements.

The Surf Bathhouse was a popular place for swimming in the summer season, as well as dances and parties. In 1909, the Young Ladies' Hospital Aid Society held a fund-raiser at the bathhouse that included a vaudeville show, a wrestling match by YMCA members, and a dance. The money raised at the event purchased necessities for charity patients. In 1910, this bathhouse was the site for the state Democratic Convention.

On December 17, 1904, the Galveston Board of Commissioners passed a resolution stating they "shall have power to regulate and determine the time and place of bathing and swimming in the waters . . . to prevent any obscene or indecent exposition, exposure or conduct." In years to come, "surf bathing" in the gulf became the number one attraction in town. One weekend in 1910, trains delivered more than 6,000 visitors from every part of Texas. Numerous events were scheduled, including a baseball game between the Galveston and Dallas teams. It was likely that a visit to the beach was also on everyone's agenda.

The Life-Saving Service patrolled the beaches to assist swimmers. Newspapers cautioned visitors, "Surf bathing on the beach should be confined within the ropes. The beach at Galveston is the safest in the world, yet one is liable to cramps or some other sudden affection while in the water . . . and therefore they should not recklessly go beyond the limits of prudence and outside the zone of assistance."

Bettison's Fishing Pier, located seven miles offshore on the North Jetty, boasted "Cool Gulf Breezes and No Mosquitos." Manager R. L. Bettison made four trips throughout the day to shuttle visitors from Chapman's Wharf to the pier, which also included a seafood restaurant.

By summer 1904, membership in the Galveston Boat and Yacht Club reached nearly 100, and the club had raised enough funds to build a clubhouse on Pelican Island. The group organized rowing parties, regattas, and boat parades, sometimes in conjunction with the annual Water Carnival. In 1908, a *Galveston Daily News* reporter visited the club and documented, "Small boys astride their fathers' backs like infant Tritons on dolphins, while the mother dolphins follow with encouraging applause, and the small boy shrieking with delight as they rise over the gently swelling waves, are scenes sketched every day with the sunset sky for background."

THE PLAYGROUND OF TEXAS

The first rowing club in Texas formed in Galveston in the 1870s, and several similar clubs soon followed. The clubs owned and managed a boathouse on the bay, organized local competitions, and participated in interstate regattas.

Central Park at Twentieth and Winnie Streets was the only planned public space in the original city plan.

The 1900 Storm destroyed Central Park's landscaping, so the Women's Health Protective Association raised funds and facilitated new plantings. Political meetings, circuses, and concerts took place in the park. Ball High School (the domed building) also used the park for recreation and Reserve Officer Training Corps drills. The city installed lights in 1911, when much of Galveston began receiving electric service.

Garten Verein, established in 1876 by a group of German businessmen, opened stock only to German speakers, but anyone could become a member of the club. The octagonal dancing pavilion shown in this image was the only structure in the park that survived the 1900 Storm. An orchestra accompanied the dance programs. Young children danced at 7:00 p.m., followed by older children half an hour later. Adults danced from 8:30 p.m. until the pavilion closed, which was sometimes as late as 3:00 a.m.

Wednesday night dinners at the Garten Verein clubhouse were a popular summer diversion for families. "There are two private dining rooms, but during the summer these are rarely used, as the grill porch is the chief delight. . . . the dining and the charm of the al fresco summers served while the band plays and the scene of merriment in the garden is an ever-moving view," noted one *Galveston Daily News* reporter. Customarily, children did not eat with adults but were served snacks through a side entrance.

The grounds of Garten Verein included a bowling alley, a croquet area, playgrounds, a bandstand, and fountains filled with goldfish. As the first site in Galveston to install underground utilities, the park was elaborately illuminated at night. Children enjoyed feeding crackers to the colorful fish in the large fountains. During the grade raising, soil from the mainland was brought in to raise the park in order to provide the best conditions for the garden's 1,500 new plantings. That project cost $21,000.

The first golf club in Texas was founded in Galveston in 1898 with 30 members. Their course was surrounded by barbed wire to keep cows from eating the grass. The clubhouse was severely damaged by the 1900 Storm. This image is the new Galveston Golf and Country Club, which opened in 1906 with a golf tournament. Although the club officially moved to 100 acres on Dickinson Bayou and renamed itself the Oleander Country Club in 1912, "renegade" members continued to golf on the island course. In 1918, the clubhouse in Dickinson was destroyed by fire, so the club was reunified on Galveston Island.

During the grade raising, Goedhart and Bates kept offices at 306–307 Trust Building. A December 30, 1904, *Galveston Tribune* article described behind-the-scenes machinations that led to them getting the contract. When calls for bids were placed, a number of companies sent representatives to survey the situation. These contractors heard rumors that Goedhart and Bates had a "new scheme they were going to spring which would knock their competitors sky high." With their own bids already prepared, but not placed, those competitors banded together to withhold their bids. They assumed that if only one bid was placed, the Grade Raising Board would be forced to decline and call for a new round. However, the group did not realize that an unknown contractor from Iowa had arrived just a few days before bids were due, completely unaware of the scheme in place. The board reviewed the two submissions and awarded Goedhart and Bates the contract.

OPPOSITE: The dredge *Nereus II* sits at one of the canal's many discharge stations. The grade-raising canal was cut through town behind the Seawall, then along sparsely populated Avenue P½.

THREE

A NOVEL APPROACH

Following the building of the seawall, the second phase of Robert, Ripley, and Noble's great plan involved raising low-lying portions of the city. The idea was to raise the land behind the seawall by 17 feet. The grade would gently slope downward at a rate of one foot every 1,500 feet until it reached 8 feet at Avenue A. A Grade Raising Commission was appointed. Members J. P. Alvey, John Sealy, and Edmond R. Cheesborough were tasked with overseeing this grand project.

Early options for the grade raising were problematic. Bringing sand from the gulf would harm the beaches; fill from the mainland would be too expensive; sand from the bay was too far away and difficult to move; and borrow pits on the West End would halt the city's only path for expansion. New York firm Goedhart and Bates presented a novel approach. Lindon Bates was a well-known dredge designer who also designed the three-lake system at the Panama Canal. His company's idea was to dig a canal across the

island. Sand taken from the canal would be used to fill the area behind the seawall. With the canal in place, Bates's newly designed dredges could remove sand from the bay and then float down the canal to a station where muddy fill would be discharged. When this dried, enough sand would remain to bring the ground to a higher level. This plan provided the extra benefit of deepening the ship channel, important for the passage of large steamships.

The *Leviathan, Nereus II, Holm,* and *Triton* sit at discharge stations along the canal. Though others, including the *Galveston*, helped at various points, these four dredges completed the bulk of the work in raising the city. The *Texas*, another dredge of the *Leviathan*'s design, was built to do the job but sank in the Atlantic on the voyage from Danzig, Germany. The *Texas* was the most powerful of the dredges intended for the grade raising. With 1,800-horsepower and a 42-inch suction, she was capable of pumping filling through her discharge pipe over a distance of one mile. With the disappointing losses of the *Galveston* and the *Texas*, the smaller *Triton* and *Nereus II* were purchased in an effort to complete the grade raising in a timely manner.

Houses and other improvements along the canal route had to be temporarily moved. As part of the deal, the Grade Raising Board agreed to pay for the cost of the move and the rental of the temporary lots where the houses were relocated. As rent for the use of the land, the board paid property taxes for the canal lots. In the spring of 1904, a total of 85 houses had to be moved from the canal right-of-way in the section north of Broadway and east of Thirteenth Street. Some property owners attempted to take advantage of the city's need. One man wanted the city to relieve him of 10 years' worth of taxes on a different property. Another thought he could get the city to build him a stable and wagon shed. Not wanting to be greedy, he declined to also ask for a horse and wagon to put into the shed. The city refused such deals and threatened to condemn the unleased properties, and eventually all the hold-outs signed.

The grade-raising canal was 3 miles long, 20 feet deep, and 200 feet across. This allowed two dredges to pass one another. Beginning at the South Jetty, at Eighth Street and Avenue A, the canal roughly followed the curvature of the seawall before turning at Twenty-second Street and following the sparsely populated Avenue P½ to its end at Thirty-third Street. Several widened sections and two turning basins (one between Thirteenth and Fifteenth Streets and the other at Thirty-third Street) allowed the dredges to maneuver in and out of the canal. The temporary waterway was also host to a pontoon, or floating, bridge at Twenty-third Street and a drawbridge at its mouth.

The first of Goedhart and Bates's dredges to arrive in Galveston was the *Holm*. To the delight of Galveston's citizens, after an eventful and much delayed journey from Germany, bathers from Murdoch's bathhouse spotted the *Holm* just after 4:00 p.m. on Sunday, June 12, 1904. In turn, *Holm* commander Capt. Thomas Knight, a Galvestonian, was welcomed back to the island by the sight of the Southern Pacific grain elevator.

Grade Raising Dredge Holm at Discharge Station in Canal.

Like the other dredges Goedhart and Bates built for this project, the *Holm* was a self-propelling, self-loading, and self-charging hopper dredge. This meant that, unlike traditional dredges, which merely dropped their cargo into place, the new design pulled in and dispensed fill at great distances through a series of pipes. The dredges would steam over or alongside a sandbank. The main engines triggered a large centrifugal pump, which pulled up the mud, about 80 or 90 percent water, and discharged it into the hoppers. With a full load, the dredge would then steam across the channel and up the canal and pipe the mixture into the grade-raising district. The *Holm* was about 160 feet long, had a 500-cubic-yard capacity hopper, and would eventually make about seven trips per day equaling about 3,500 cubic yards of fill.

Eighth Street and Avenue A, the canal's entrance, was already the location of the inner portion of the South Jetty. Unfortunately, the jetty was home to a railroad trestle that supplied Fort San Jacinto, whose batteries were being rebuilt. Before the canal could be dug, a 150-foot drawbridge had to be built at its entrance so that the fort, on the East End Flats, would not be cut off from its supply source. To speed the bridge's construction, the pile driving crew building its foundation had both a day and a night shift. Specifications required that the bridge could be opened or closed in 10 minutes. It was built to hold the weight of trains with heavy loads of rock and other material to be used in the fortification's reconstruction. Above top, the drawbridge is opened to allow a small tugboat into the canal. When opened, the grade-raising dredges could pass through. The dredges suctioned sand from the bay and then entered the canal with a fresh load of fill, discharging it before exiting to continue the process. Above bottom, the dredge *Holm* sits in front of the closed drawbridge. When closed, the bridge permitted government trains to pass to and from Fort San Jacinto. The large building at left is the Negro Hospital, which opened in 1902.

The *Holm* soon began the difficult work of digging the canal. The entrance to the canal was a graveyard of large jetty rocks and old railroad tracks scattered by the 1900 Storm. Whenever the dredge encountered these obstacles, it would have to shut down and back away. Derricks were used to clear the obstructions. The *Holm*'s many setbacks made the citizens of Galveston anxious and unhappy. To accelerate the progress, the Charles Clarke Company, using Bowers Southern Dredging Company vessels, was subcontracted at a rate of 7¢ per cubic yard to help the *Holm* dig the canal. Clarke's dredges, including *No. 4*, *No. 6*, and *No. 7*, were tasked with making the canal ready for use by Goedhart and Bates's larger dredges. Above top, Clarke's dredge, the *George Sealy*, is working to deepen the turning basin between Thirteenth and Fifteenth Streets. In the above bottom image, one of the dredges' massive cutters can be seen.

With the Clarke dredges preparing the canal, the *Holm* was finally able to make its first trip to the bay as a hopper boat. It took its first load of sand from the edge of the channel on November 18, 1904.

The introduction of the canal created a thin peninsula of land that stretched between the canal and the seawall from Thirty-third Street to the eastern end of the island. The area around the seawall between Twenty-first and Twenty-fifth Streets was a popular amusement district, and it was intended to be among the first areas filled so not to interfere with the tourist season. To provide access, workers built a pontoon bridge across the canal at Twenty-third Street. This bridge was only intended for pedestrians. Streetcars and wagons would still have to go the long way around to the connection at Thirty-third Street.

The canal was still being built when new dredges arrived from across the Atlantic. The *Galveston*, the second of Goedhart and Bates's dredges to arrive, had three times the capacity of the *Holm*. At 250 feet long and 40 feet across, the hopper dredge could hold 1,500 cubic yards and had a 1,200-horsepower capacity. Her 42-inch pipe allowed a mass of material four times that of the *Holm*'s 21-inch pipes.

The third Goedhart and Bates dredge to arrive on the island was the aptly named *Leviathan*. At 9:10 a.m. on January 25, 1905, she arrived in port flying the Dutch flag under the charge of a Holland native. The *Holm* and the *Galveston* had arrived under American flags thanks to American skippers. The same size as the *Galveston*, with the same 1,500-cubic-yard capacity, but with a lesser, 800-horsepower engine, the *Leviathan* was built in Kinderdyk, Holland, by L. Smit and Son, the same firm that constructed the *Holm*.

After only a few months of work, the *Galveston* was determined unable to meet its builder's guarantee. While built of the same design, the *Galveston* failed to do the amount of work accomplished by the *Leviathan*—a problem attributed to faulty construction. Problems with the hull meant that the *Galveston* loaded at a much slower rate than intended. The *Galveston* was sent away to Mobile, Alabama, to be rebuilt. For a little while, the enormous task of filling in the island was left to the *Leviathan* and the tiny *Holm*.

Unlike its sister ship, the *Galveston*, the *Leviathan* far exceeded expectations. A December 1905 article in the *Galveston Daily News* proclaimed "Leviathan a Wonder." Its builders had guaranteed the vessel would pump fill a distance of 1,500 feet, but it was actually pumping a distance of 4,102 feet. Workers tested its limits and had hopes of reaching 6,000 feet, or four times its guarantee. The boat averaged five loads of fill from the bay each day when only four were expected, sometimes managing six or even seven loads on days when it was only necessary to pump a short distance onto the island.

Cave-ins were an issue along the canal. Wooden levies were built in an effort to keep the canal's sides from collapsing. The canal's entrance was closer to the seawall than was comfortable, and on at least one occasion, a cave-in caused the wall's supports to become visible. Both tourists and locals found watching the dredges at work to be a popular attraction. Unfortunately, the preferred viewing spot was often the ridge of sand alongside the canal. The city requested people not watch from that ridge but rather stand on top of the seawall for a safer view.

The canal was also the sight of a number of accidents. On one occasion, the *Galveston Daily News* reported that a mail carrier and his horse fell into the canal and made a narrow escape. They managed to make it ashore, but the mail bag was a near casualty. The bag, "partially filled with mail, could not swim but could float, and while the bag got wet, the mail matter escaped but slight damage. But the experience was one that is not to be considered along the line of surf bathing." On another date, a boy nearly drowned after the flatboat he and a friend rode sank. W. H. Laycock complained, "The canal at places is full of children swimming and floating about in old boats, boxes and, in fact, anything that will hold them." Among the less fortunate was 22-year-old Emil Maas, a crew member on the dredge *Holm*, who drowned after he fell out of a skiff and was drawn beneath the *Holm*.

With the *Texas* lost at sea and the *Galveston* a failure, Goedhart and Bates scrambled to procure other dredges in an effort to hasten the fill process. Two dredges, the *Nereus II* (above top) and the *Triton* were hastily purchased to provide back up for the *Holm* and the *Leviathan*, already hard at work. Completing Goedhart and Bates's Galveston fleet, the two new additions had practically the same capacity as the *Holm* but were a trifle wider and had a different suction pump mechanism. The dredge above is collecting sand from the bay. The one below is floating high, having already ejected its fill.

Houses at Twenty-fourth Street and Avenue M sit on stilts awaiting fill. In addition to providing a solid backing for the seawall, the grade raising was intended to keep storm water from ever reaching a level that would be dangerous to life or property. The new grade would also provide sufficient elevation for drainage and sewerage that had not previously been possible. More than 2,000 buildings had to be raised, including churches, schools, 1,226 cottages, 413 one-story houses, and 162 stables. In addition, water mains, gas lines, sewer lines, streetcar tracks, streets, sidewalks, fences, shrubs, trees, gardens, and outhouses also had to be raised to the new grade.

OPPOSITE: The house at center, located at 1319 Twenty-fourth Street, belonged to Edmond R. Cheesborough, secretary of the Grade Raising Board.

FOUR

A CITY ON STILTS

With the canal underway and dredge boats in place, the grade raising could begin in earnest. The dredges went into the bay, collected sand and water, entered the city through the new canal, moored at one of its many discharge stations, and piped new fill throughout the town. In 1906, a Ball High student described the scene as such:

> The dike, or embankment, which serves to keep the water within its limits is in need of repairs, and men are busy patching it up with straw and mud, assisted by the moon's pale light and the flare of torches. Other men are busily arranging the gigantic pipes, through which the water is to come, and a crowd of spectators, some sitting, some standing on the board walk which extends from one stilted house to another, watch the preparations.
>
> Soon the whistle of the dredge sounds, which is the signal that they are ready to start the pumping, and in a few moments the water and sand begins to gush from the pipes, slowly at first, but gradually gathering force until the muddy water is leaping, tossing, roaring as it sweeps in torrents beneath the houses. One of the joints becomes slightly loosened by the force of the water, and a stream spurts upward some fifteen or twenty feet. Men wearing rubber hipboots wade about endeavoring to make the pipes secure, and, in the attempt, are almost carried off their feet, so great is the current.
>
> After a time the water comes more slowly and with less force. Soon it subsides altogether and only the soft, slushy mud is to be seen. All is still where fifteen minutes before was a rushing, swirling expanse of water.

Marks were placed throughout the city to show residents the height of the planned grade raising. Permanent bench marks were to be placed at every other street intersection with temporary marks in between. The above photograph shows the neighborhood with the filling in progress. In the two images at left, a man points to a painted white line on a telephone pole before and after the fill. This house was on Avenue P, between Twenty-fifth and Twenty-sixth Streets.

With the white marks as a guide, thousands of buildings were raised on stilts above the future ground level. Some homeowners took the opportunity to make improvements on their houses and properties. This house received a new porch and fence. The top image shows how commonplace this engineering feat would become. Though their home sits 10 feet in the air, a child casually peers out of the window while a man holds a toddler leaning against one of the piers supporting the house.

St. Patrick's Catholic Church, located at Thirty-fourth Street and Avenue K, sustained a great deal of damage during the 1900 Storm. The tower collapsed through the building, and the interior was ruined. After repairs to the building were made, it was raised five feet using 700 jack screws. One hundred men worked to raise the church, one-half inch at a time, for 35 days. Once the correct height was reached, a new concrete foundation was poured. Some thought this was an impossible feat, but it was accomplished by the H. Sheeler Company of Chicago without cracking the main walls or damaging the interior. Church services continued throughout the whole process. At 3,000 tons, it was the largest of the 2,156 structures raised during this period.

In the years of repair and rebuilding after the 1900 Storm, many property owners had ignored or misread property lines. Fences and buildings encroached upon public sidewalks and alleys. The necessary removal of these improvements during the grade raising gave officials an opportunity to alleviate this problem. Engineers resurveyed property lines, giving owners a template to use. Some property owners made cooperated efforts to uniformly adjust houses and fences for the sake of neighborhood beautification. These images show houses near Twenty-fourth Street and Avenue N.

The island was raised in two- to three-block sections. Levees, or banks of dirt, from 2 to 10 feet high were placed around each section to be filled. A drainage ditch was left open on the lower side to allow the excess water to drain back into the canal or down to the bay. As the many who were surprised by sudden and stagnant flood could attest, these drains did not always work. This house is at Twenty-eighth Street and Avenue P.

Grade Raising at Galveston

In the early days, drainage was an issue and the grade-raising districts were prone to flash flooding. A December 1904 *Galveston Daily News* article described how fill water imprisoned a group at a friend's house. A woman, her children, and a servant were attending a wedding in the grade-raising district. Clark dredge boat *No. 7* was in the vicinity but not in operation when they left for the wedding, so there was no concern for the water. The article read, "It was a great surprise when after the party broke up, it was discovered that the house was surrounded with water" at least a foot and a half deep and that escape was not possible.

Three sizes of iron pipes were used to discharge fill. The biggest was 42 inches across, large enough for a small child to walk through or a couple of grown men to comfortably sit in. The 42-inch pipe came in 12-foot lengths, each weighing 2,000 pounds. This size was used by the *Leviathan,* the *Galveston,* and the ill-fated *Texas.* Additionally, 21- and 33-inch pipes were used.

This before and after scene at the 3000 block of Avenue O shows buildings were not the only things that needed to be raised. The fence, at left, has been raised several feet in anticipation of the fill. The woman with the umbrella stands on one of the many raised platforms and walkways built to allow travel from one building to another, or to the streetcar in her case. When the fill was still wet, the mosquitoes, already a problem on the island, became unbearable. This neighborhood, once lush with trees and other greenery, became barren and dusted with sand. Unhindered by vegetation, the sand flew freely at the hint of a breeze, and windstorms are common in Galveston.

GRADE RAISING SCENE. PUMPING IN THE FILLING.

This image of a pipe leading directly from a dredge at a nearby discharge station shows the violence with which the fill erupted from the pipes. Anything raised without secure supports would be demolished in its path. Workers discovered that some items, such as streetcar tracks, could not be braced ahead of the fill in any manner that would allow them to stay aloft.

The fill consisted of up to 95 percent water, which was intended to drain back into the canal. Some people complained that a higher percentage of sand would have hastened the grade-raising process. In a letter to the *Galveston Daily News* dated July 23, 1904, C. W. Trueheart, M.D., protested that the water took too long to drain away, thus endangering the health of those in the area and causing damage to the vegetation as a result of prolonged exposure to the saltwater. Goedhart and Bates maintained that the high level of water was required to force the fill long distances through the pipes, as well as to wash the sand away from the mouth of the pipe after it had been discharged. The water also kept the fill fairly level, thus minimizing the need for scrapers.

The image above shows temporary walkways at Seventeenth Street and Avenue K. The walkway at right was at Twenty-eighth Street and Broadway. Wooden walkways throughout the city allowed people to walk between buildings without wading through the muddy fill. The haphazard placement of these walkways often resulted in creative paths. An April 14, 1905, *Galveston Daily News* article described how one of their reporters, "unacquainted with the conditions, found himself trapped. He had come to a point where the sidewalk ended. Beyond was mud and water, and behind him a large discharge pipe was throwing out great quantities of filling, generously mixed with water. To get to the car line, his destination, a block further to the north, seemed impossible without wetting his feet. It was at this juncture that a resident came along and, with the true Samaritan spirit, directed him to cross the street, walk back upon the elevated sidewalk, pass through a corner grocery and let himself down upon the dike, which led down an intersecting street to the Avenue L car line. It was simple enough, barring the danger of making a misstep and landing in the water, but it required a knowledge of how to do it."

A streetcar passes along the east side of Twenty-fifth Street and Broadway. In the days when automobiles were just becoming widely available, streetcars were a popular method of getting around town. City Commissioner Valery E. Austin noticed that the Grade Raising Board allowed their engineer $12.50 a month for streetcar fare. He and the other commissioners later voted to allow the city's own engineer $10 per month, as he was "every day almost called to different portions of the city to look after work" and had been paying the fares out of his own pocket. A last-minute amendment to the motion allowed the superintendent of the electric light department $10 per month for streetcar fare or horse feed!

The streetcar companies were in a constant struggle to keep running amid the controlled chaos of the grade raising. With an uncrossable canal through the heart of the system, rail lines and schedules were constantly being shuffled and moved to accommodate passengers traveling through the areas being filled. Five of the Galveston Electric Company's 10 lines had already been cut in half by the canal. This image shows the Broadway esplanade looking east from about Twenty-sixth Street.

Streetcar tracks raised prior to the fill were in serious danger of being washed out by the intensity of the watery mud gushing from the pipes. After a period of trial and error, the decision was made to allow the sand to fill around the tracks until nearly or entirely above the rails, and then the track was jacked up a few inches at a time. The sand was so soft that crews had problems with the jacks sinking six inches before they could raise the track even one inch. Rapid shoveling was needed to ballast the track up before it would sink again. These workers are a Twenty-second Street and Broadway.

Levees were built to ensure the new fill did not escape. These houses at Thirty-fifth Street and Broadway were at the north edge of the grade-raising district and, therefore, were not to be filled. The large two-story house at left still exists but has since been turned to face Thirty-fifth Street.

An earthen levee surrounds the house at right. In areas where the fill was to be low, such as this neighborhood at Twenty-eighth Street and Broadway, property owners protected their yards from the destructive saltwater with temporary levees. The saltwater and sand was not conducive to vegetation, and efforts were made to protect trees and allow for new growth. Some property owners raised their front yards with material taken from the rear part of their lots. Others chose to remove their topsoil, store it in bins or set it on platforms, and replace it once the new fill had been pumped in.

The man in this photograph, taken at Twenty-eighth Street and Broadway, is standing partly on a fill pipe and partly within a wooden barrier intended to save a young palm tree from the saltwater's wrath. Just inside his fence sits a pallet holding a stack of bricks, possibly intended for use as a walkway. Residents were asked to remove all shell, brick, and concrete sidewalks and keep them for the final covering.

With landscape being destroyed daily, citizens teamed up in an effort to re-beautify their city. A driving force in this effort was the Women's Health Protective Association (WHPA), founded in March 1901, only months after the devastating storm. As the city's first Progressive Era civic group, their goal was to build a better community. Their projects included protecting the city's cemeteries, schools, and parks, as well as ensuring a sanitary environment during the grade raising.

The WHPA organized fund-raisers to buy plants for the beautification of Galveston. One of their most successful efforts was the Third Annual Horse Show, held at Twenty-seventh Street and Avenue N. The show drew a large crowd to watch races, listen to brass bands, and visit display booths. Thanks to the popularity of the automobile, the annual event ended after 1910 as there were simply no longer enough horses to participate in the events. Before that, the proceeds raised thousands of dollars to purchase plants and trees for the city. In just one year, the women planted 8,000 sycamore, cottonwood, elm, oak, and hackberry trees, as well as 2,500 oleanders and 2,000 palms. The WHPA planned and maintained the landscaping for about 10 years, until the work was turned over to the city government. These women's efforts can still be seen throughout Galveston.

These images show the house at 1804 Thirty-fifth Street during and after the grade raising. As the era of mud, water, and large dredges floating through town came to a close, Goedhart and Bates had lost a quarter of a million dollars on the grade-raising project.

SeaWall and
Beach at Galveston.

By 1910, great strides had been made to protect the island city. The seawall reached Fifty-third Street and would be further extended. The grade raising continued on the outskirts of the city. On January 1 of that year, a *Galveston Daily News* article explained that "practically every bit of marsh and every mosquito-breeding water hole in the entire city has been wiped out. In this list is included Coles Bayou, McKinneys Bayou, Woollams Lake and the mud bridge slough, a large body of water west of Forty-fifth street and north of Broadway." However, the downtown business district would remain at its old level. The entire project cost Galveston $6 million.

Galveston was the best natural harbor in Texas. Dredging in the late 1800s made it into the state's first deepwater port with access for large steamships. Revenues from the shipping business were instrumental in Galveston's recovery after the 1900 Storm.

OPPOSITE: Ships from all over the world docked in Galveston to unload imported produce and merchandise and to load cotton and other cargo for export. The busy port was filled with sounds of screeching machines, steamship horns, and the whistles of tugboats.

THE LARGEST PORT WEST OF THE MISSISSIPPI RIVER

Founders of Galveston envisioned the town site as a natural harbor, and their efforts to build a vital shipping center were successful. Prior to the 1900 Storm, Galveston was the business center of Texas, known as the "Wall Street of the Southwest" or the "New York of the Gulf." Warehouses stuffed with imported wholesale goods supplied stores throughout Texas and the entire Southwest. Numerous railroad companies transported freight and passengers. Galveston functioned as the region's principal banking center thanks to its numerous wealthy citizens. The city boasted the finest hotels and restaurants west of the Mississippi River.

The 1900 Storm did relatively little damage to the port, and shipping resumed as soon as the railroad

connection to the mainland was restored. During the time Edworthy photographed Galveston, the town was concentrating its resources on building defenses for survival, which included the seawall and the grade-raising projects. Galveston vied for commercial survival as well, competing with rivals Houston and Texas City. Activity at the port actually surpassed pre-storm levels. One additional benefit of the grade-raising project was the deepening of the port, which allowed the passage of larger ships. As World War I began, Galveston was the leading cotton port in the world, the third largest exporter of wheat, and an important sugar import center. It was common for general merchandise store owners to be paid with crops, which was often cotton. This led the owner into the cotton brokerage and transportation businesses as well. Galveston also became a major port of entry for thousands of immigrants. From 1906 to 1914, nearly 50,000 newcomers arrived in Galveston from Europe and Asia. This influx of worldly goods and people gave Galveston a sophisticated character unlike any other Texas town.

Grain elevators (right) were an important part of port activities. The first grain elevator stored and loaded grain for export in 1875. In the early 1900s, the grain market fluctuated. In 1912, European grain harvests were poor while Galveston's exports were record-breaking. Author James Hanna remembered, "At Pier 14 stood the great grain elevator, and if there was any grain to be loaded, its loud whistle would be blown at seven in the morning, at noon, and one at five o'clock in order to regulate the activities of the workmen."

The Galveston Wharves documented 1,672 vessel arrivals in 1910. Dockworkers unloaded goods for rail shipment throughout the Southwest. Longshoremen used hand trucks to load cargo from warehouses to the docks, where winches hoisted the bundles onto the ships. One witness described the scene: "All this was accompanied by the rattle and screech of block and tackle and the chugging escape of steam as the small engines up on deck turned the winches. Sometimes the cargo nets would be filled with 500 pound bales of cotton or heavy crates of machinery or slabs of red copper."

The Galveston Cotton Exchange, once located at Twenty-first and Mechanic Streets adjacent to the *Galveston Daily News*, was organized in 1873 to facilitate the shipping of cotton from the interior of Texas to the port of Galveston and beyond. It was the first exchange established west of the Mississippi River and the third oldest in the country. This enabled Galveston to become the largest worldwide exporter of cotton grown in the southwestern United States in the early 1900s.

E. C. Worrall and Company was listed as a member of the Galveston Cotton Exchange and Board of Trade in 1910. The gentlemen in this image are grading cotton to determine its value based on fiber length, uniformity, diameter, strength, maturity, color, and the amount of foreign matter (like leaves and sticks) mixed in the cotton.

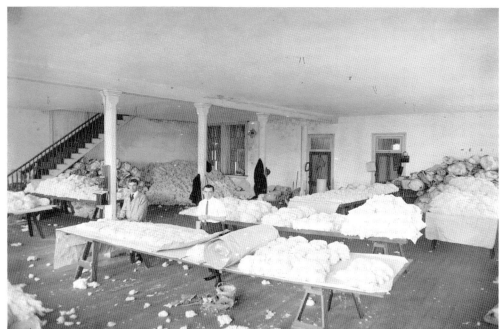

Cotton was one of the first major agricultural products grown and exported in the United States. Until the Civil War, two-thirds of Texas cotton was shipped through Galveston. The record number of bales shipped out of the port was 4,045,495 in 1912–1913. One *Houston Daily Post* reporter visiting the busy docks in 1913 noted, "The steam-winches puffed loudly, the ropes strained noisily, the negroes chanted melodiously as 1000s of bales of cotton were hoisted aboard the ships."

Mallory Docks - Galveston.

The Galveston Wharf Company made port improvements to accommodate the Mallory Line, established in August 1866 with service between New York City and Galveston via New Orleans. Mallory's Texas Line soon emerged as the dominant carrier on that route. By 1905, their schedule included nine steam vessels, all named after Texas rivers, that made ports of call in New York, Texas, Alabama, Georgia, and Florida. The 1877 pilot boat *Mamie Higgins* is in the left foreground of this image. In 1904, the vessel was completely rebuilt and continued to serve in the harbor as a relief boat for the steamer *Texas*. Pilot boats guided arriving ships through the harbor.

S.S. CONCHO, MALLORY LINE.

The SS *Concho* of the Mallory Line regularly made trips between New York and Galveston. According to the *New York Times*, in June 1909, Capt. L. Young reached Galveston after a trying experience at sea. The crew discovered a serious leak on the vessel when it was about 150 miles from Galveston. When pumps were not able to keep up with the incoming water, the captain wired for assistance. However, suddenly, the leak stopped and the pumps caused the water to recede. Upon arriving in Galveston with a damaged cargo, divers examined the ship's hull. They found a large fish had lodged itself in the 8-inch hole! Captain Young believed that the ship had struck a submerged wreck, and he credited the fish with saving the SS *Concho*.

The SS *Pilar de Larrinaga* was built in 1902 by Larrinaga and Company, Liverpool. As World War I approached, on May 4, 1917, this merchant ship was torpedoed by a German submarine and sunk while en route from Galveston to Manchester Port, England. Twenty men were killed.

The USS *Galveston* was commissioned by the navy in 1904 and conducted missions on all seas. On April 10, 1905, at a ceremony held at the 1894 Grand Opera House, the ship was presented a silver service tea set by citizens of her namesake city. One unique mission of the ship included escorting the remains of American Revolutionary hero John Paul Jones from France to the Naval Academy Chapel in July 1905. After it served for many years, the U.S. Navy decommissioned the ship in 1930 and replaced it with a new ship of the same name.

Schooners like the *Carrie Winslow*, built in 1880 in Maine, and the *James Pierce* were becoming a rare site at the ports of Galveston by the early 1900s. Massive steam-powered ships were quickly replacing sailing vessels. However, private captains of sailing schooners still transported smaller cargo or fished along the U.S. and South American coasts. As late as 1924, sailing schooners were used for coal shipments from Philadelphia because their freight costs were cheaper than steam lines. One *Galveston Daily News* reporter wrote about the rarity of sailing ships: "Just as the old order must always give way and be absorbed by the new. And, who knows but what the steam vessels that displaced them might not be themselves displaced by the motor ships with their exhaust pipes in lieu of the time-honored stacks just as the lofty masts of the old sailing vessels have been replaced by the short cargo masts of the present ocean carriers?"

LARGE STEAMER LOADING AT GALVESTON.

In September 1904, the SS *Penrith Castle* left Galveston for the European ports of Antwerp and Havre loaded with various cargos, such as more than 100,000 feet of pine lumber, more than 1,200 barrels of cottonseed oil, 698 bales of cotton, and 288 tons of zinc ore. The ship's cargo also included 10 walnut logs valued at over $2,500. In addition, the ship transported a small number of passengers, who were sometimes recorded with distinguishing marks for identification. In 1911, a 21-year-old male laborer named George Huber arrived on this vessel and was noted to have a scar under his right eye.

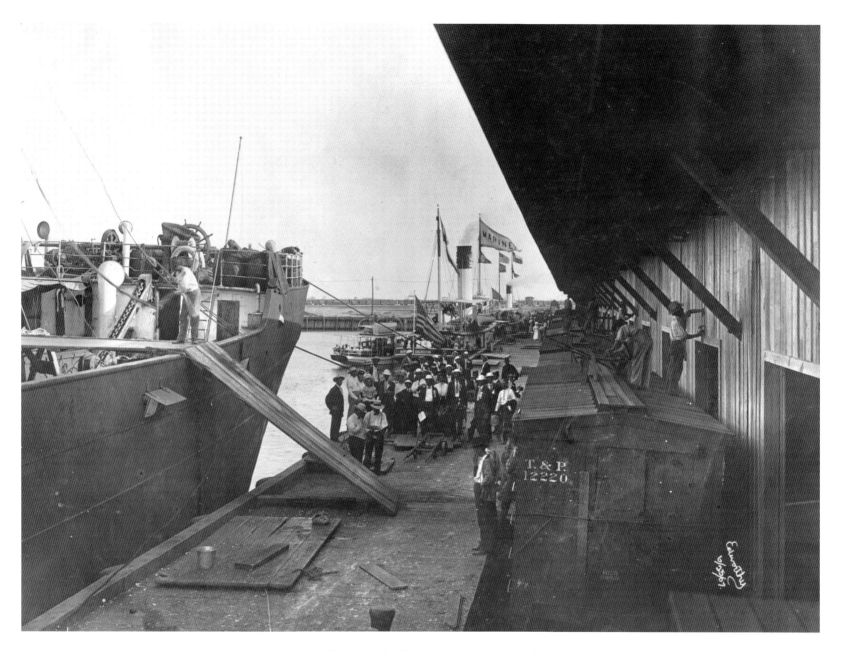

On the back of this image of the SS *Manchester Port*, photographer Edworthy wrote, "How freight is handled direct from rail to water haul." This ship, built in 1904, was owned by Manchester Liners, Ltd. Although their ships primarily transported cotton, they could accommodate a small number of passengers.

Mosquito Fleet, Galveston.

Pier 19, in use since the times of pirate Jean Laffite, remains the home of the shrimp boats known as the Mosquito Fleet. The name originated from the insect-like appearance of the boats' nets hanging to dry, as well as their light, quick speed. The traditions of over 100 nationalities mingled among the fishermen in these wharves. Seasonally, the boats brought produce and other foods from the mainland to Galveston. These small boats could maneuver the narrow, shallow waters of the rivers and bayous, reaching places that did not have access to railways. At times, the Mosquito Fleet was a floating market with a wide variety of goods, including fruits, vegetables, rabbits, eggs, chickens, and hay. The fleet contributed to regional growth of small farming communities. However, the new causeway completed in 1912 caused the fleet to weaken.

When the first large shipment of bananas arrived in Galveston in January 1899, it caused so much excitement that police were used to keep the crowds under control. Ripe bananas were sold to Galveston and Houston wholesalers, while the remainder of the shipment was loaded onto refrigerated railcars and transported to cities all over the Southwest. In 1907, as a peddler was selecting a stalk of bananas from wholesalers Pabst Brothers on the Strand, he encountered a deadly stowaway. As he reached to cut the stalk, a 4-foot-long tropical "snake shot out its ugly head within an inch of his hand." Reports stated the man was scared speechless but managed to point and wave to draw attention to the problem. A crowd gathered to kill and confirm the death of the poisonous snake.

Photographer Zeva B. Edworthy left Galveston aboard the *Livingstone Bergen* in 1908 for an excursion to Tabasco, Mexico. Edworthy is seated under the "L" wearing a white cap and bow tie. The group toured the Rio Grijalva aboard the photographer's launch *Mary Frances*, built by the Galveston Launch and Motor Company. On the return trip, the steamship brought back a load of bananas.

Between 1906 and 1914, about 50,000 immigrants arrived in Galveston. Many were Germans, Czechs, and Jews, although numerous other nationalities and religions were also represented. While most immigrants moved to other parts of Texas and the Southwest, some remained in town to settle and establish businesses. Galveston became known as the second Ellis Island. Some immigrants arrived with the support of the Jewish Immigrants' Information Bureau and the Methodist Immigration Information Bureau. By 1914, the outbreak of war in Europe restricted all immigration into the United States.

Although the origin of these passengers is unknown, a large number of immigrants arriving in Galveston from 1907 to 1914 came as part of the Galveston Movement (also known as the Galveston Plan). This plan was organized to help Jews flee from Eastern Europe, especially Russia. In spring 1907, the Jewish Immigrants' Information Bureau opened under the direction of local rabbi Henry Cohen. About 10,000 immigrants came to the United States through Galveston as a part of this program. The typical routine for incoming Jewish immigrants was to undergo a medical exam and baggage inspection at port before they were loaded onto wagons that took them to the Information Bureau. They were given a wholesome meal and had the opportunity to bathe, write letters, and read Yiddish newspapers. They received their railroad tickets and food for the trip to their final destinations. Typically, employment had been prearranged in towns throughout the western United States.

Immigrants awaiting Inspection at Galveston.
Photo by Edworthy

Galveston's busy seaport was plagued by epidemics of yellow fever in the late 1800s. The city built a maritime quarantine station to isolate incoming ships in order to prevent the spread of disease. For years, incoming immigrants were processed in warehouses meant for cargo storage, and many families spent the night in the railroad depot before boarding trains to their final destinations. The numbered cards pinned on the newcomers correspond to ship passenger records.

Signs reading "Baggage Checked Here" are written in English, German, and Czech.

A few hours after the dredge *Triton* left Madeira, the crew discovered a stowaway hiding in one of the discharge pipes on deck. The 15-year-old boy, who desired to live in America, was placed in confinement. When the vessel arrived in Galveston on December 22, 1905, the boy was shipped back to the Portuguese island.

The lively seaport was filled with ships from around the world. These crewmen, possibly from Southeast Asia or North Africa, appear to be grinding food for a meal. The seawall and grade-raising projects required a large influx of laborers.

Behind this Rosenberg fountain, several of which were placed around town for people and animal use, is the Galveston Union Railroad Station, located at Strand and Twenty-fifth Streets. It was built in 1897 and demolished in 1931. Galveston had been served by numerous railroad companies since the initial Galveston, Houston, and Henderson Railroad was chartered in 1853, and this station served passengers traveling on all the lines. People could go all over the country from Galveston, which was unprecedented in the Southwest.

This view looks northwest from Twentieth and Winnie Streets. St. Mary's Cathedral School
for Girls dominates the left foreground.

OPPOSITE: This view depicts downtown Galveston looking down Twenty-third Street from
Strand Street. Several hotels, including the Tremont and Palmetto, along with stores and
offices, line the bustling streets.

SIX

SCENES AROUND TOWN

A canvass of the real estate and building situation in Galveston reveals a good, healthy and steady increase. There is nothing of a boom character in any department of the city's growth; just a gradual improvement of trade and building conditions. In many instances there would be seen valuable and permanent improvements under way but for the grade raising operations. There are perhaps hundreds who are patiently awaiting the time when that work will be completed so that they may build.

—*Galveston Daily News*, 1904

The grade-raising project progressed through town from the seawall to Broadway, leaving out the business district. Understandably, there were very few large buildings constructed during this time.

The Rosenberg Library was the most significant exception. Some of the hardest hit institutions were the churches and schools located in the area to be filled. These groups worked hard to raise funds in order to have their buildings elevated or rebuilt in the wake of grade raising. Those who invested in real estate improvements demonstrated confidence in the future of Galveston.

The building of Ashton Villa significantly determined the fate of Broadway as the grand boulevard of Galveston. Completed in 1859 by wholesale merchant and railroad company president James M. Brown, it was the first stately residence to face Broadway. It had advanced conveniences like closets, indoor plumbing, gas lighting, and heating. By this period, Ashton Villa was occupied by his wife, Rebecca Ashton, and his daughters, Bettie Brown and Matilda Brown Sweeney. During the grade raising, the home was not jacked up. However, the family purchased clean, white sand from the island's west end for their yard in order to become more level with the area south of them, which had been raised by the city. Topsoil was also brought in to cover the sand and provide for landscaping. Today the iron fence surrounding the property is short because about 3 feet of the fence is buried underground, along with part of the basement.

Scene on East Broadway, Galveston, Tex.

Walter Gresham (1841–1920) and wife Josephine Mann's home, built in 1892, was located just out of the range of the grade-raising project at 1402 Broadway. Colonel Gresham was a prominent lawyer, legislator, and railroad executive and was also a member of the Deep Water Committee. This committee facilitated one of the most significant improvements to the harbor, which deepened the waters to allow for larger vessels. Gresham also worked with the county to facilitate the construction of portions of the seawall.

West on Broadway from 15th, Galveston.

The home on the right was completed in 1906 for Isaac H. Kempner (1873–1967) and his wife, Henrietta Blum. Kempner was instrumental in establishing the commission form of government and securing funds to rebuild the city after the 1900 Storm. His home was one of the few large residences built on Broadway in the early 1900s. The home was the location for many events involving Henrietta Kempner, who was active in the Red Cross and the Parent-Teacher Association.

Daniel W. Kempner (1877–1956), cotton merchant and rancher, built this home in 1908, following his marriage to Jeane Bertig. After a four-month-long wedding trip in Europe, the property was purchased from land owned by Ursuline nuns for the construction of a new house. This location, on Avenue O, established that neighborhood as a new upscale area. The construction of these Kempner homes represents a new generation of wealth investing in Galveston's future.

Looking northwest on Broadway and Twenty-third Street, this is the edge of the area raised with fill. The home of Peter J. Willis, who owned one of the largest mercantile businesses west of the Mississippi River, is on the left. Another mercantile owner, cotton broker, and insurance company president, Civil War colonel John D. Rogers, built the home behind the Willises'. The Frosh house is on the right. The only building in this picture that remains today is the Rosenberg Library, which is considered the most significant new structure built in this period.

The Rosenberg Library opened in 1904. The funds for the structure were from the bequest of Henry Rosenberg (1824–1893). By November, a substantial branch for the black community was also opened at Central High School with 2,000 books and plans for additional volumes.

From its opening, Rosenberg Library served the community with free lectures, exhibits, and other educational programs. Librarian Frank Patten secured speakers from universities nationwide. In March 1910, the newspaper publicized two lectures by Dr. Charles Zueblin, who was published and well-versed in the concepts of ideally planned cities with healthy, educated societies. Careful planning for the future was on the minds of many. Dr. Zueblin promoted the "Galveston Plan," a form of commission government that the town had adopted after the 1900 Storm. He felt that Galveston was a fine example of a 20th-century city. Other library programs were designed for youths, complete with projected stereopticon slides.

This home, located at 1717 Postoffice Street, was built in 1890 for Elise C. Michael. During this period, families often did not maintain their own horse and buggy at home. Instead, they paid a livery stable downtown to provide transportation. James Hanna remembered, "Each morning, promptly at 8 o'clock a Negro boy would drive the horse and buggy to our house and secure it to a hitching post at the curb. Then going around to the back of the buggy he would unfasten a bicycle with specially made iron towing arms and return to the livery stable to make another delivery. At whatever time of the day or night that Father had no further use for the vehicle he would telephone the livery stable and in a few minutes the boy would appear."

The congregation of the First Baptist Church raised funds to build a new church to replace the one that had been destroyed. The new building, located at Twenty-second Street and Sealy Avenue, was completed in 1905.

One marble statue stood untouched among the ruins of the original Sacred Heart Catholic Church after the 1900 Storm. This photograph shows the new sanctuary at 928 Fourteenth Street that opened in 1904, with the surviving statue placed atop the dome. The exterior of the building was in progress at the time this photograph was taken. As sections of the grade raising were completed, dirt was left behind for those wanting to level uneven yards. The dirt in the center of this image is presumably for that purpose.

The Central Christian Church, at Twentieth Street and Avenue K, was at the center of the city's grade-raising project. In 1905, the congregation decided that if their building had to be raised, then they would take the opportunity to expand the size of the church to accommodate Sunday school rooms and a kitchen.

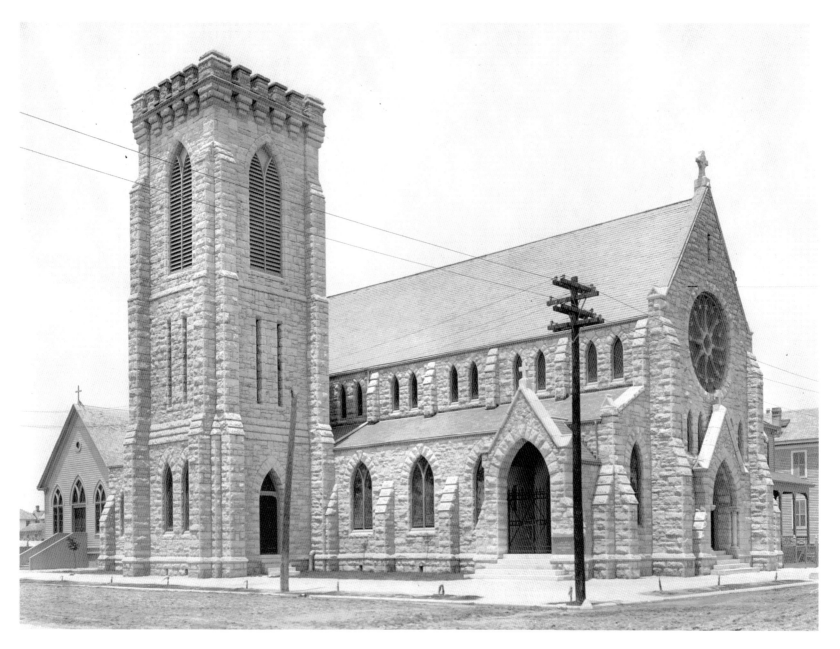

In 1895, the bequest of Henry Rosenberg funded the construction of the Grace Episcopal Church, designed by architect Nicholas Clayton at Thirty-sixth Street and Avenue L. The church was a refuge for survivors of the 1900 Storm and the site of the first wedding after the storm. Dr. Joe Gilbert married Daisy Thorne surrounded by mud and debris. In 1907, in preparation for the city grade raising, the church was raised four feet with hand-turned jacks by contractor John Egert. His company was known for its ability to raise buildings without damage.

In its founding years, Galveston had difficulty finding an adequate source for fresh water. Rainwater was caught in cisterns, but it was not enough for the booming population. Attempts to dig wells resulted in an inadequate water supply filled with sulfur, lime, and salt. Finally, in 1895, a pipeline was completed that pumped water from wells in Alta Loma on the mainland. This image depicts the Galveston Water and Electric Light Station, which was designed by Charles W. Bulger in 1904 at Thirtieth Street and Avenue H, after the original building was destroyed. It is one of the oldest city water supply centers still in use in the United States.

PHOTO by Edworthy.

The "Alamo" School.

The Alamo School, on the west end of the city at Thirty-eighth Street and Broadway, was one of four white grade schools within the early Galveston Public School System, which also included two schools for black students. In 1906, the enrollment of 782 students caused an overcrowding problem at Alamo. The boundaries of the schools were adjusted to accommodate future growth. Part of the overcrowding problem at the schools was probably due to the influx of people providing labor on the construction projects. One schoolboy remembered attending school with the children of the dredge boat and pipeline workers. He stated that he learned many new words that year, as the new classmates had been taught to "curse and swear as well as their parents." That same year, the city health physician requested that all classrooms be fumigated to control insects and diseases such as tuberculosis and scarlet fever.

Galveston established a free public school system in 1881 in accordance with a new state law. Funded by philanthropist George Ball, Ball High School, located at Twenty-first and Ball Streets, opened in 1884. It quickly became known as one of the finest schools in the Southwest. In June 1905, at the commencement ceremony, school board president I. Lovenberg addressed the crowd, "We may well feel proud of the fact that our city has not only acquired much fame throughout the country by the successful efforts of her citizens in recuperating from the great disaster of the year 1900, but that it has also retained its position as the leading city in our State in matters of public education."

Ball High School gained an athletic department in the early 1900s. Sports included football, basketball, track, baseball, and tennis, several of which included male and female teams. According to The Review, the school's yearbook, the object of the athletic program was "not to hinder the progress which they are expected to make in their studies, but on the other hand, to add interest, to inspire confidence and to enable the pupils to surmount difficulties." The school's athletic association awarded felt letter "Bs" for members based on their participation and skill improvement. The football team in this period was just forming, and there were difficulties securing games with other teams, so they primarily played among two student teams, named the Purples and the Golds. Eventually, the team traveled for out-of-town games, including competitions with rival Houston High School.

The Galveston Orphan's Home was originally founded in 1878 and received funds from the bequest of Henry Rosenberg for construction in 1895 at Twenty-first Street and Avenue N. Although no children were harmed in the 1900 Storm, the building suffered major damage. A three-day bazaar was organized at the Waldorf-Astoria Hotel in New York to fund the repairs. On November 27, 1902, the building was reopened. Nine boys and one girl returned to live at the home after being temporarily placed in Dallas. The *Galveston Daily News* stated, "It will be great comfort to the mothers who have children to know that the little ones who have no mother and no home are provided with everything their little hearts could wish for." Typically, a child could not be admitted into the home unless one or both parents were deceased and remaining family members agreed to abide by visitation rules.

The Letitia Rosenberg Home for Aged Women was established in 1888 with an all-female board. The building, at O½ and Twenty-fifth Streets, was funded by the bequest of Henry Rosenberg in 1895. At least 51 elderly women lived there between 1896 and 1917, most of whom were foreign born. During the grade raising, this massive building was raised and the front steps were reconfigured. When fill was pumped in, water continually seeped through the concrete walls and into the basement. The problem was somewhat alleviated by filling from a different direction.

John Sealy Hospital, 815 Strand Street, opened in 1890. Along with the medical college, this institution founded the significant traditions of medical education and research in Texas. During the grade raising, on July 15, 1904, the *Galveston Daily News* reported that a crowd had gathered under the shade trees at the hospital to watch progress as the *Holm* dug the canal. As sand caved in at the head of a canal, the onlookers were quite surprised when the ground gave way right under their feet. There was a rushed scramble to get to firmer ground, but no one was hurt.

In 1891, the Ashbel Smith Building, commonly called "Old Red," was designed as a companion building to Sealy Hospital. It was the first medical college in the state, and it remains the oldest existing medical school west of the Mississippi River. The college expanded greatly in this period in the number of students, faculty, and projects. In 1912, the Department of Histology and Embryology was organized with the first female faculty member, Dr. Marie Charlotte Schaefer. One of her most significant accomplishments was the identification of the hookworm infestation in the southern United States.

URSULINE CONVENT

The first bishop of Texas requested Ursuline nuns from New Orleans establish a school for girls, which opened in 1847 at Twenty-seventh Street and Avenue N. Before the Galveston public school system was established in 1881, citizens depended on Catholic schools for their children's education. The original campus covered 10 acres and included a dorm, monastery, and chapel. The convent grounds suffered greatly with storm damage. Raising funds for repairs and then for the subsequent grade-raising effort was a hardship on the institution. The grounds were so low that an elevation of six feet was required. The Grade Raising Board planned to brick up a portion of the windows and reconfigure the entrance and the basement steps. They also filled in near the building with dry dirt instead of pumping in muddy water in an attempt to prevent the basement from flooding.

On April 9, 1907, the *Galveston Daily News* reported this fire on Strand Street between Twenty-fourth and Twenty-fifth Streets. The fire began from the burner on a melting pot of glue located in a furniture store. The destroyed buildings included the Sealy Building, the Richard O'Rourke Building, and the J. H. Hutchings Estate Building. These contained the offices of the Gulf, Colorado, and Santa Fe Railway, the Jewish Immigrants' Information Bureau, and other shops. As firemen fought the raging downtown fire, embers floating through the air started other small fires on homes several blocks away.

In August 1909, the Midget Bar at 2220 Postoffice Street, was the scene of a raid by the Texas Rangers. A week of investigations uncovered poker, craps, roulette, and dice games running in rooms upstairs. The Rangers began their Sunday raid with a surprising bomb explosion. They arrested 13 men in the midst of a poker game. Raids of other saloons found many newly built gambling rooms in preparation for the large crowds expected during the Cotton Carnival.

This view of downtown looks west from the 2200 block of Postoffice Street. The Young Men's Christian Association (YMCA) occupied the first building on the left. The YMCA conducted physical training classes for youths that included tumbling, Indian clubs, basketball, and other games. Classes always ended with a refreshing swim in the pool. By 1911, the grade-raising project had been completed, the construction of the new causeway had begun, and numerous businesses were also underway with new improvements. The Tremont Hotel, farther west in this image, underwent major remodeling, and the YMCA installed a new bowling alley in the basement.

THE "BAY BRIDGE" WHICH CONNECTS GALVESTON ISLAND WITH THE MAINLAND.

Before the causeway was completed in 1911, passengers and freight arrived in Galveston by rail. Trains were forced to a slow crawl across the bay because of the weak bridge. There had also been a wagon bridge connecting the 2-mile stretch from the island to the mainland, but it had been destroyed in the 1900 Storm and not rebuilt. Constructing a more substantial, weatherproof link had been considered for many years, but railroad companies feared it would compete with their services. Most Galvestonians supported the project after the 1900 Storm because it would provide a quick route of escape upon the arrival of another deadly storm, as well as increase tourism and decrease the cost of importing produce and other goods.

According to one Ball High School student in favor of the new causeway, "This coming in closer contact with the outside world will, without a doubt, benefit Galveston, in that new ideas will permeate the minds of our citizens, which will gradually raise this city in population and distinction before the eyes of the world."

The causeway opened May 25, 1912, with a ceremony led by Texas governor O. B. Colquitt. The new causeway had lanes for railcars, automobiles, and pedestrians. With the growing popularity of automobiles and the completion of the Galveston-Houston Interurban rail, the numbers of people visiting Galveston steadily increased throughout the 20th century.

Despite the destruction behind the seawall (seen here at Sixteenth Street), the wall survived the 1915 storm relatively unscathed. Today the seawall remains, guarding the island city. (Courtesy of J. V. Bowen.)

EPILOGUE

Human history becomes more and more a race between education and catastrophe.

—H. G. Wells

Since the first section of the seawall was finished in 1904, the wall has grown with the city until it was finally completed in 1963. Rock groins were added in the late 1930s to alleviate the erosion of the island's beaches. Sand must be replenished after each storm that passes or makes landfall on the coast. Subsidence has also caused the wall to sink. It now stands at 16 feet, instead of the original 17 feet.

On July 21, 1909, a hurricane struck Galveston with a storm tide that rose 10 feet above average sea level. Later the 1915 hurricane proved more powerful than the infamous 1900 Storm. This storm sent a schooner over the seawall and into Fort Crockett. Battering waves, weighing about 1,728 pounds per cubic yard, damaged concrete behind and on top of the wall. The 1915 hurricane, which also destroyed portions of the 1912 causeway, proved beyond a doubt that the seawall and grade raising had been worth the effort.

Without the seawall, the city would have suffered severe damage when Hurricane Carla hit in 1961 and Hurricane Alicia in 1983. The seawall held back the gulf, and the storms showed very clearly that building beyond the seawall was risky.

As I look at the seawall, I have to wonder what if Hurricane Carla had not made landfall over 120 miles away in Matagorda Bay, but much closer in Brazoria or Galveston County? What would have happened to the city of Galveston, had the height of the storm surge been over 20 feet? Winds from Hurricane Carla blew at a sustained 85 miles per hour. If the storm had directly hit Galveston, winds would have been closer to 150 miles per hour. Building codes would have failed, and it is possible that the seawall would have become a reef on the ocean's floor under such extreme forces of water and wind.

Today we must remember that storm in 1900 and how the city recovered. Even though the seawall shows some cracks from being exposed to the forces of nature, it still protects. In 2005, Hurricane Rita threatened Galveston and the coast as a category five storm, more powerful than any other in the known history of Texas. Those living in the Galveston Bay area were very lucky the storm did not follow the forecasted track, but instead made landfall along the Sabine River, well east of the island. The storm passed through a cool eddy that weakened its winds. Rita, as forecasted, would have made landfall on the unprotected area of the island, near San Luis Pass, bringing its full force over the entire island.

In conclusion, the citizens should be proud of what their ancestors accomplished at the turn of the 20th century. Although the city had been bankrupt, the leaders decided to risk everything and rebuild, and they succeeded without federal assistance. Their efforts made Galveston great; they made history that I am proud to write about here with this collection of images, saved for us by the Edworthy family and the Galveston County Historical Museum. I do hope that those who read and study this book have indeed been educated.

Very humbled,
Lew Fincher
Hurricane Historian, Galveston County Historical Commission and
Vice President, Hurricane Consulting, Inc.

One unfortunate consequence of the grade raising could be found in a number of sunken buildings after the 1915 storm. In some areas, the ground had not yet settled properly, causing scenes such as this. Despite such disastrous images, the seawall and grade-raising projects proved to be a huge success. Only eight lives were lost in Galveston, compared to the 6,000 to 8,000 who had perished in the 1900 Storm. (Courtesy of Mildred Theiler.)

Clockwise from upper left: The 1915 storm damaged the Mosquito Fleet, decimated Murdoch's and the other bathhouses along the beach, collapsed the approaches to the newly completed causeway, and caused considerable damage to the area where the Electric Park stood. Yet again, a storm could not stop Galveston. The Mosquito Fleet survives, still housed at Pier 19. Murdoch's has been rebuilt several times over the years. The current building is home to a tourist shop. The causeway was repaired and is still in use for the trains that make their way on and off the island. The Electric Park later became the site of the Buccaneer Hotel with its roller coaster and amusement area. (Clockwise from upper left, courtesy of J. V. Bowen; Albert B. Davis Jr.; George, Lisa and Deven Renner; and Catherine V. Matin.)

The Great SEA WALL and Boulevard

Galveston Today, A City Raised High Above the Sea.

Photo by Reverman

According to historian David G. McComb, Galveston's "struggle for survival against nature through the application of technology represents the strongest tradition of Western civilization. Galveston's response to the great storm of 1900 was its finest hour, and demonstrated that rationality and determination can prevail. This is the lesson that Galveston teaches all visitors who come to the edge of time, stand on the seawall, and gaze in wonder upon the vastness of the sea."

SELECT BIBLIOGRAPHY

Baker, T. Lindsay. *Building the Lone Star: An Illustrated Guide to Historic Sites*. College Station, TX: Texas A&M University Press, 1986.

Bates, Lindon W. Jr. "Galveston—A City Built Upon Sand." *Scientific American*. July 28, 1906.

Beasley, Ellen, and Stephen Fox. *Galveston Architecture Guidebook*. Houston, TX: Rice University Press, 1996.

Burka, Paul. "Grande Dame of the Gulf." *Texas Monthly*. December 1983: 160–169, 216–225.

Cooper, H. S. "The Story of the Galveston Grade Raising—From the Street Railway Point of View." *Street Railway Journal* Vol. 27, No. 19: 752–756.

Davis, Albert B. Jr. Galveston's Bulwark Against the Sea: History of the Galveston Seawall. Rev. ed. Galveston, TX: U.S. Army Engineer District, Galveston, 1961.

Davis, W. Watson. "How Galveston Secured Protection Against the Sea." *The American Monthly Review of Reviews*, 1906: 200–205.

Eisenhour, Virginia. *Galveston: A Different Place, A History and Guide*. Galveston, TX: self-published, 2003.

"Fish Saves A Liner." *New York Times* Vol. LVIII, No. 18,761. June 6, 1909: 1.

Fox, Stephen. "Broadway, Galveston, Texas." *The Grand American Avenue*: 1850–1920. Jan Cigliano and Landau Sarah Bradford, eds. The Octagon. San Francisco, CA: Pomegranate Artbooks, 1994.

www.newspaperarchive.com

Galveston County Historical Commission, resource and state marker files located at the Galveston County Historical Museum, 2219 Market Street, Galveston, TX.

Hanna, James S. *What Life was Like When I was a Kid*. San Antonio, TX: The Naylor Company, 1973.

www.tshaonline.org

Kelso, Margy. *A Glance Back: The First Century of the Galveston Country Club*. 1998.

Kessler, Jimmy. *Henry Cohen: The Life of a Frontier Rabbi*. Austin, TX: Eakin Press, 1997.

McComb, David G. *Galveston: A History*. Austin, TX: University of Texas Press, 1986.

"Raising the Grade of Galveston." *The Engineering Record* Vol. 51, No. 10 (1905): 284–285.

"Raising the Grade of Galveston." *The Railroad Gazette* Vol. 36, No. 1 (1904): 6–8.

"The Relocation of Public Service Systems During the Grade Raising of Galveston, Tex." *The Engineering Record* Vol. 54, No. 11, 1906: 299–302.

The Review. Ball High School Yearbook 1905–1907.

Scardino, Barrie, and Drexel Turner. *Clayton's Galveston, The Architecture of Nicholas J. Clayton and His Contemporaries*. College Station, TX: Texas A&M Press, 2000.

Turner, Elizabeth Hayes. *Women, Culture, and Community: Religion and Reform in Galveston, 1880–1920*. New York: Oxford University Press, 1997.

Walden, Don. "Raising Galveston." *Invention and Technology*. Winter 1990: 8–18.

ACROSS AMERICA, PEOPLE ARE DISCOVERING SOMETHING WONDERFUL. *THEIR HERITAGE.*

Arcadia Publishing is the leading local history publisher in the United States. With more than 4,000 titles in print and hundreds of new titles released every year, Arcadia has extensive specialized experience chronicling the history of communities and celebrating America's hidden stories, bringing to life the people, places, and events from the past. To discover the history of other communities across the nation, please visit:

www.arcadiapublishing.com

Customized search tools allow you to find regional history books about the town where you grew up, the cities where your friends and family live, the town where your parents met, or even that retirement spot you've been dreaming about.